Weather

Weather

HERON BOOKS

Published by
Heron Books, Inc.
20950 SW Rock Creek Road
Sheridan, OR 97378

heronbooks.com

Special thanks to all the teachers and students who
provided feedback instrumental to this edition.

Printed in the USA

30 April 2022

At Heron Books, we think learning should be engaging and fun. It should be hands-on and allow students to move at their own pace.

To facilitate this we have created a learning guide that will help any student progress through this book, chapter by chapter, with confidence and interest.

Get learning guides at
heronbooks.com/learningguides.

For teacher resources,
such as a final exam, email
teacherresources@heronbooks.com.

We would love to hear from you!
Email us at *feedback@heronbooks.com.*

IN THIS BOOK

Chapter 1

What Is Weather?

Every day the air outside feels a little different than the day before. The air may be warmer or cooler than the day before, or it may be moving faster or slower than it was the day before.

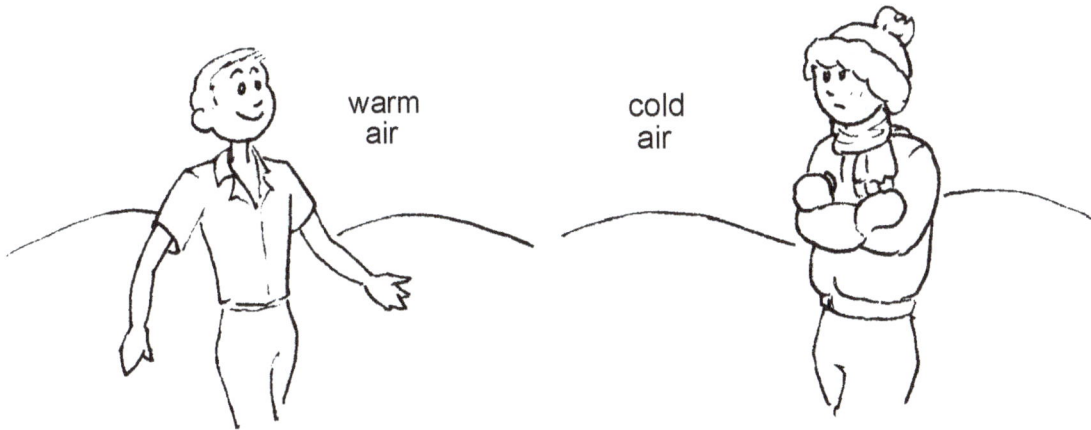

warm air

cold air

One day it may be warm.

Another day it may be cold.

One day it may be calm.

Another day it may be windy.

Some days the sky looks different than on other days. Some days it is blue and clear.

Other days it is gray and cloudy, and maybe it rains.

How the air outside feels, how the sky looks, how much sunshine there is, and what is going on in the air is the **weather**.

The weather is all around us. And it is always changing. It is never exactly the same on any two days.

People often talk about the weather, because everyone who lives in the same area shares the same weather. The weather is also interesting, because it is different every day. Sometimes it is the way we want it, and sometimes it isn't.

Everyone living in the same area shares the same weather.

Chapter 2

Sunshine

Sunshine is the light and heat that comes from the sun. Sunshine is the most important thing that affects the weather. Sunshine warms the air and the ground. It warms your body, too, if you stand in it. Sunshine helps plants grow, and gives us light to work and play by.

People usually feel the weather is nicer when the sun is shining.

When the weather is cloudy or rainy, the clouds block the sunshine from reaching the ground.

When the weather is very warm, sunshine may not be so nice because it is too hot!

Sunshine causes the weather to change. When sunshine warms the air, this can cause the wind to blow and the clouds to form. Wind can bring the clouds and rain, or it can blow the clouds away and bring dry weather.

So, what is the main cause for all the kinds of weather changes we live with?

Sunshine!

LET'S DO THIS!
Feel the Sun

To do this activity, you will need

- sunny day
- lamp with a light bulb

Steps

1. On a sunny day, find a place where you can stand with the sun shining on your face. Feel the heat from the sun.

2. Turn around so the sun does not shine on your face. Notice the difference.

3. Feel three things that are in the sun and see if they are warm.

4. Feel three similar things that are not in the sun, and notice the difference.

5. Go inside and find a lamp where you can feel the heat of a light bulb. Guess how many light bulbs it would take to replace all the heat the sun is giving to your building. Write down this number, and write why you decided it would take that many.

6. In writing, tell why sunshine is the most important part of weather. Then write your idea of what the weather would be like if there were no sunshine.

7. Show another person your writing from steps 5 and 6.

Chapter 3

Warm Air and Cool Air

Sometimes the air outside is warm and comfortable. Other times it is quite cold and you need a jacket to stay warm.

How do we know how warm or cool it is? One way to tell is to go outside and feel the air. But if we want to know exactly how warm or cool the air (or anything else) is, we can measure the temperature of it.

Temperature is a word that means how hot or cold something is. Something that is hot has a high temperature. Something that is cold has a low temperature. If we measure the temperature of the air, we can tell exactly how hot or cold it is.

The temperature of the air is an important part of weather. The temperature of the air can be cold even if the sun is shining. And the temperature of the air can be high even if it is cloudy or rainy.

warm air

cold air

To measure how hot or cold the air is, we use a tool called a **thermometer**. *Thermo* means temperature, and *meter* means measure. A thermometer measures the temperature in numbers called **degrees**. The word **degree** really just means "a small step." A degree on a thermometer is a small step in temperature.

Some thermometers look like this:

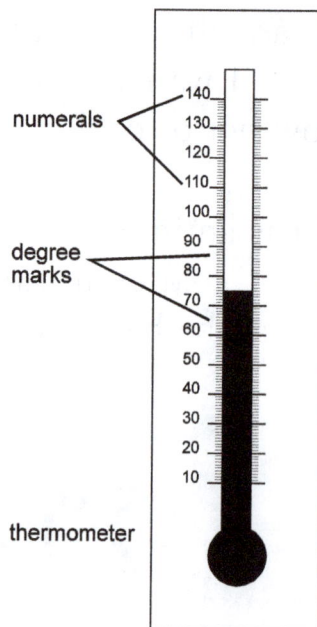

numerals

degree marks

thermometer

There are two different **scales,** or sets, of degrees often used to measure temperature. They are named after the men who invented them.

One is called the **Fahrenheit** scale (or F for short).

The other is called the **Celsius** scale (or C for short).

Of course, they measure the same temperatures—they just give them different names. For instance, normal room temperature is about 70 degrees on the Fahrenheit scale. That same temperature (in the same room!) measures 21 degrees on the Celsius scale. It is sort of like the difference between using feet or meters to measure distance.

Some thermometers show Fahrenheit degrees and some show Celsius degrees. Some even show both.

A thermometer tells you how warm or cold something is by showing what number of degrees of temperature it measures. For example, the temperature of your body is quite warm. A thermometer would show your body temperature to be about 99 degrees F, or 37 degrees C. If the air outside was this temperature, it would be a very hot day.

When water freezes, a thermometer shows a temperature of 32 degrees F or 0 degrees C. When the air is around this temperature or lower, people say it is "freezing." You need a warm jacket to go outside when it is freezing.

When a thermometer shows a temperature of 70 degrees F or 21 degrees C, it is nice weather.

When a thermometer shows a temperature of 100 degrees F or 38 degrees C, it is hot weather.

By measuring air temperature with a thermometer, you can tell how warm or cool the air is and how comfortable you will be in this air. You can tell if you will need a jacket or a sweater to go outside.

You can tell a lot about the weather by measuring the air temperature with a thermometer. Air temperature is a big part of weather.

LET'S DO THIS!

Air Temperature

To do this activity, you will need

- refrigerator with a freezer

Steps

1. Put your hand close in front of your mouth and blow your breath on your hand. The air you feel from your breath is close to 100 degrees F.

2. Wave your hand around in the room you are in and feel the air. That air is around 70 degrees F.

3. Go to a refrigerator and put your hand inside it for a few seconds. The air in the refrigerator is usually about 40 degrees F. Now put your hand in the freezer part of the refrigerator and feel the air there. The air in the freezer is about 20 degrees F.

4. Go outside and feel the air. Decide what temperature the air outside is closest to: the air from your breath, from your room, from the refrigerator, or from the freezer.

5. Decide your answers to these questions:

   a) What temperature do you think the air is?

   b) Is the air warm or cool?

c) What kind of clothes would you wear if you were going to stay outside for a while?

6. Write your answers to these questions, and show another person.

Chapter 4

Reading a Thermometer

Just as a clock will tell you what time it is, a thermometer tells you what the temperature is. When you look at a clock or thermometer and understand what it's telling you, that's called **reading** it.

Many thermometers have a dial and a pointer, kind of like a clock with only one hand. They are quite easy to read; you just have to tell what numeral the pointer is pointing to.

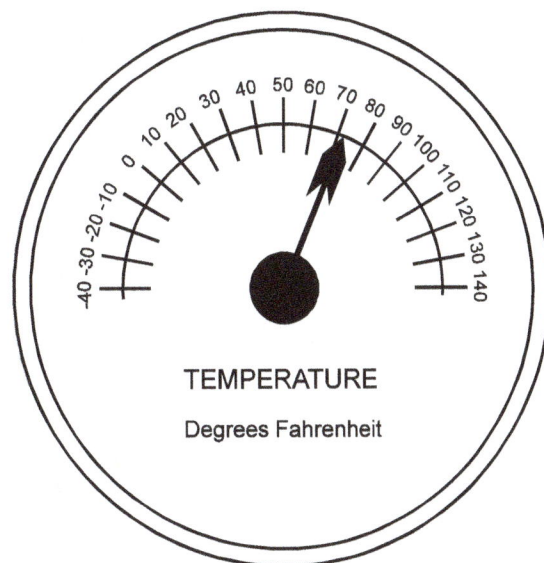

TEMPERATURE

Degrees Fahrenheit

Other thermometers are made of a thin glass tube with a little bulb at one end and a liquid inside. The liquid moves up and down inside the tube as the temperature of the liquid changes. The top of the liquid goes up when the temperature gets warmer, and goes down when it gets colder. It takes a while for the liquid to move up or down, so you might have to wait a minute for it to change.

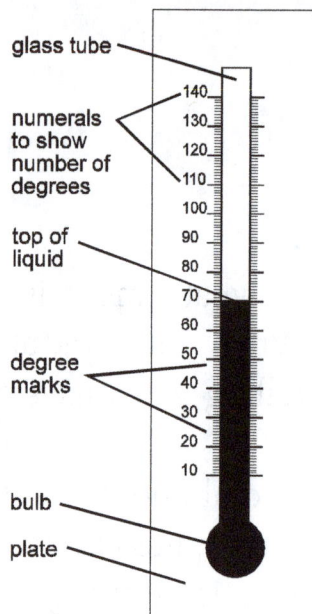

glass tube

numerals
to show
number of
degrees

top of
liquid

degree
marks

bulb

plate

140
130
120
110
100
90
80
70
60
50
40
30
20
10

The glass tube is usually attached to a plate with a row of numerals on it. (Sometimes the numerals are marked right on the glass tube.)

To find out the temperature, you read the numeral where the top of the liquid is. The thermometer drawn above shows a temperature of 70 degrees. The top of the liquid is at the 70 mark.

Between the numerals on the plate of the thermometer (such as 50, 60 and 70) there might be several more marks. These are kind of like the small marks between the inch marks on a ruler. Usually there is one mark for each degree of temperature. This means that

18

there can be 10 marks for the numerals from 50 to 60, and 10 more marks for the numerals from 60 to 70, and so forth.

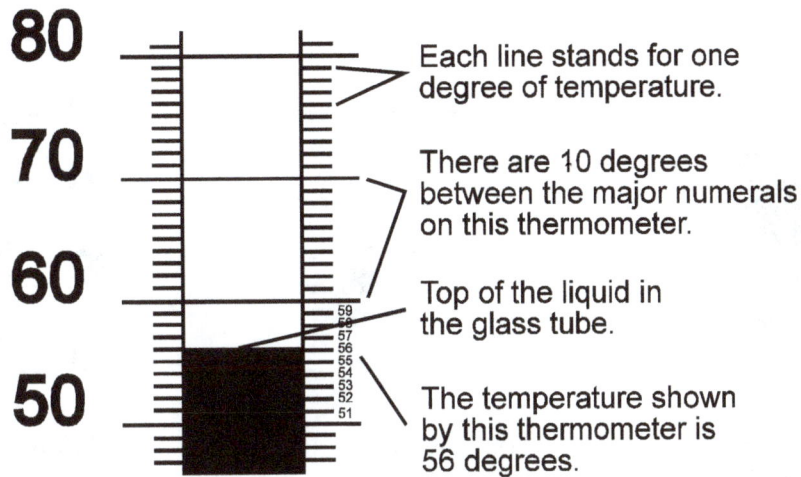

80

Each line stands for one degree of temperature.

70

There are 10 degrees between the major numerals on this thermometer.

60

59
58
57
56
55
54
53
52
51

Top of the liquid in the glass tube.

50

The temperature shown by this thermometer is 56 degrees.

Since each line marked on the thermometer stands for one degree, you can read the temperature shown on the thermometer quite accurately. First read the nearest numeral that is below the top of the liquid. Then starting there count the number of degree marks up to the top of the liquid.

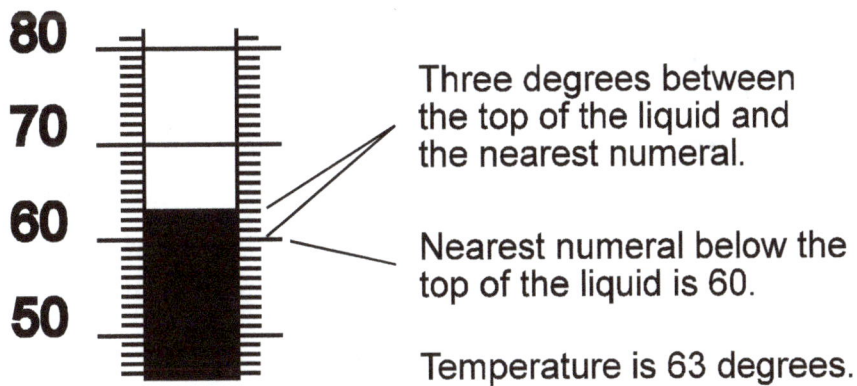

80

70

Three degrees between the top of the liquid and the nearest numeral.

60

Nearest numeral below the top of the liquid is 60.

50

Temperature is 63 degrees.

For example, if the thermometer shows a temperature like the one pictured above, then you can see that the nearest numeral below the top of the liquid is 60. You can also see that there are 3 marks between 60 and the top of the liquid. So the temperature shown by the thermometer is 63 degrees.

Here are other examples.

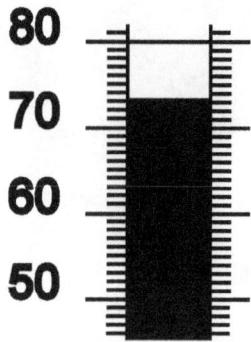

80 70 60 50
This thermometer shows 73 degrees.

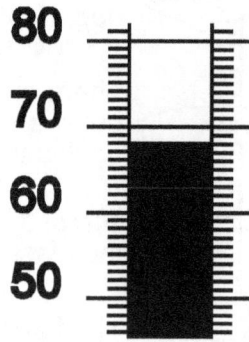

80 70 60 50
This thermometer shows 68 degrees.

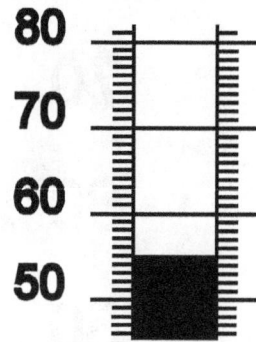

80 70 60 50
This thermometer shows 55 degrees.

Not all thermometers show 10 marks between the main numerals. Some have marks only every 2 degrees, and you have to count between the marks to get the right temperature. So you have to look at the thermometer to see how many degrees you can count for each mark.

You read the degree scales for both Fahrenheit and Celsius thermometers the same way. But you need to notice which kind of thermometer you are reading. This is because 28 degrees on a Celsius thermometer is quite warm, and you could go outside without a jacket, but 28 degrees on a Fahrenheit thermometer is freezing! Many thermometers have both of these scales marked on them, so you can pick either one.

LET'S DO THIS!

Reading a Thermometer

To do this activity, you will need

- glass thermometer

Steps

1. Get a glass thermometer and find and touch (or point to) each of the following parts:

    a) the plate

    b) the degree marks

    c) the numerals

    d) the glass tube

    e) the liquid

    f) the top of the liquid

    g) the bulb

2. Read the thermometer to see what the temperature is in the following places. (Be sure the top of the liquid has stopped moving when you read the temperature. This will take about one minute.)

Write down where you took the temperatures and what the temperatures were.

a) on the floor

b) as high as you can reach in the room

c) in your hand

d) under your armpit

e) touching a window

f) in your pocket

g) in your hair

h) in a hallway

i) between two fingers

j) on your desk

3. Show your temperatures list to another person.

LET'S DO THIS!
Measure Air Temperature

To do this activity, you will need

- glass thermometer
- record sheet with labeled rows and columns as shown in the example at the end of this activity.

Steps

Do this activity once in the morning and once in the afternoon.

1. Go outside with a thermometer, and feel the temperature of the air. Guess what the temperature is.

2. Before you measure the air with your thermometer, here are some tips:

   - Let the thermometer stay in the air for at least one minute before you read it.

   - When you take your measurement, be sure to keep the thermometer out of direct sunlight, and don't touch it yourself. This way you can be sure you are measuring the air temperature and not the heat from the sun or your body.

   Now measure the air with the thermometer. Notice how close your guess was.

3. On your Weather Record sheet, find the line for day 1. Write down the temperature you measure, and the date. The weather record sheet has two lines for each day. The line marked AM is where you write the morning temperature and the line marked PM is where you write the afternoon temperature.

4. Decide how you will schedule your air temperature checks so you do it each day you are on this book, once in the morning and once in the afternoon.

5. The first time you do this, show another person your Weather Record sheet and explain your schedule.

Example Weather Record Sheet

Day No.	Date AM/PM	Air Temp.	Wind Type	Wind Direction	Weather Types	Cloud Types	Rain Meas.	Storm Types	Notes
1	Date AM								
	PM								
2	Date AM								
	PM								
3	Date AM								
	PM								
4	Date AM								
	PM								
5	Date AM								
	PM								
6	Date AM								
	PM								
7	Date AM								
	PM								
8	Date AM								
	PM								
9	Date AM								
	PM								
10	Date AM								
	PM								
11	Date AM								
	PM								
12	Date AM								
	PM								
13	Date AM								
	PM								
14	Date AM								
	PM								

Chapter 5

Wind

Wind is nothing more than moving air. You can make a small wind by blowing air out of your mouth.

When the air outside is moving, the wind is part of the weather.

Two things about wind are important to weather—the speed of the wind, and the direction of the wind.

SPEED OF THE WIND

The speed of the wind means how fast the wind is going.

The speed of wind here is fast.

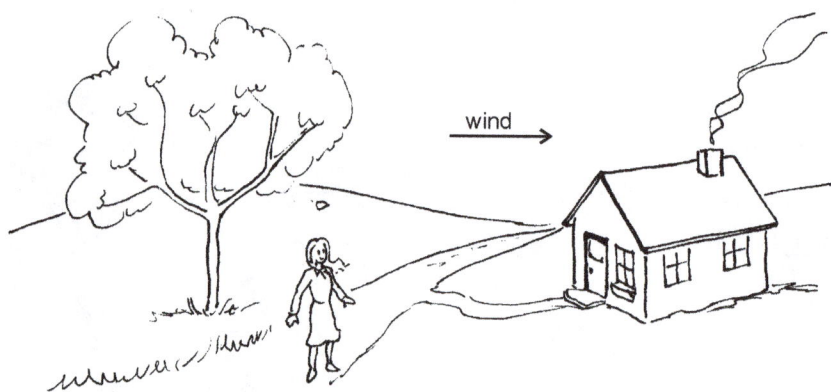

The speed of wind here is slow.

The speed of the wind affects how nice it is to be outside. When the wind is not blowing at all, we say the air is **calm**. Calm air is usually nice to be in. When the air is calm, it is hard to feel the air unless you move through it.

When air is calm, leaves are still and smoke goes straight up.

When the air moves slowly, this is called a **breeze**. When a breeze blows, leaves move and shake on trees, and smoke bends as it rises. A breeze feels good on a hot day because the moving air cools you as it blows by. You can easily feel the air when a breeze blows. A breeze is generally comfortable to be in.

When the air is moving fast, it is called a **wind**. So *wind* has two meanings. It can mean "any moving air outside," or it can mean "fast moving air." When a fast wind blows, trees bend and sway and smoke is quickly taken away by the wind. A wind will pick up leaves and papers, and carry them along with it.

If the air is cold, a wind makes it feel even colder. Your body gets cold when you stand in a cold wind. When the air is hot, a wind sometimes can make it feel even hotter.

A strong wind pushes on your body and may make it hard to walk. A wind can blow your hat off, or even knock you down if it is moving fast enough. When a wind blows, we say that the weather is "windy."

DIRECTION OF THE WIND

The second thing about wind that is important to weather is the direction of the wind. This means which direction the wind is blowing *from*, not the direction it is blowing to.

So, if the wind is blowing from the west to the east, we say the direction is from the west or just west. A wind from the north is called a north wind. A wind from the south is called a south wind. If you said it was a southwest wind, that would mean the wind was blowing from the southwest to the northeast.

You can tell which way the wind blows by seeing which way things in the air move.

For example, the direction that trees bend and the direction that smoke and dust move can tell you which way the wind is blowing. If you watch carefully, sometimes you can see the clouds move and tell which way the wind is blowing them. You can also feel which direction the wind is coming from by turning your body and feeling the wind as it hits your face.

We can often tell from the direction of the wind what the weather will be like later that day or the next day. Wind blowing from one direction may mean it will rain later on. But wind blowing from another direction might mean sunny weather is coming. By watching the wind and weather closely, you can learn how to tell what kind of weather will soon come.

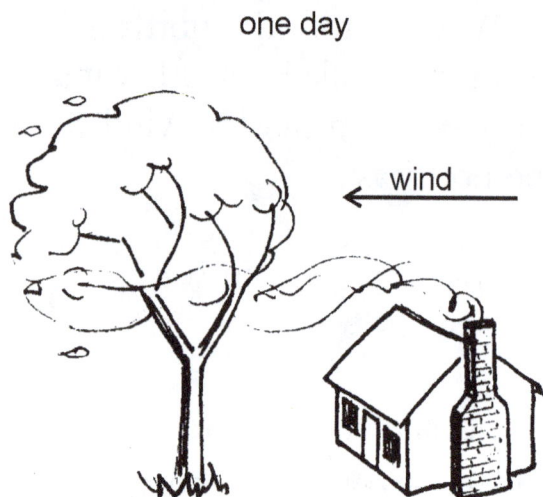

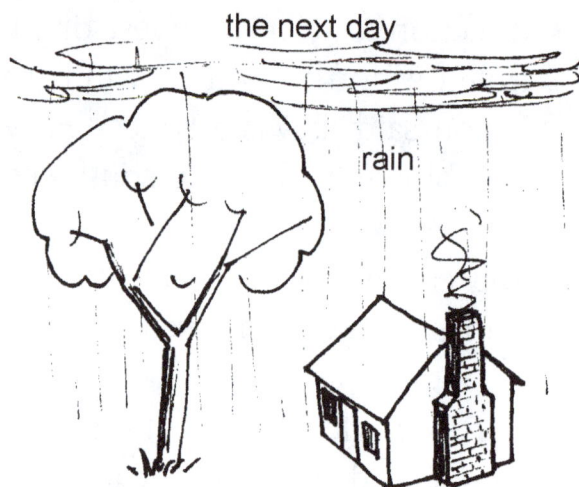

one day

the next day

wind

rain

one day

the next day

wind

We'll learn about how that works later in the book.

HOW SUNSHINE MAKES WIND

Sunshine makes wind. To understand how that works, we have to notice some things about air. The most important thing to notice is that when air gets warmer, it goes up. You can tell this by looking at the flame from a candle, or any fire.

The fire makes the air hot. This heated air does not spread out evenly, or go in just any direction. It goes up (unless another wind pushes it around). You can tell that by the way the flames go or holding your hand a safe distance above the flame and feeling the warm air going up.

When the heated air goes up, cooler air nearby comes in to replace it. This makes a little wind near the fire. You may not be able to feel this little wind by a candle, but sometimes, like when you have a pretty big fire in a fireplace, you can notice this wind easily.

heated air
going up

cooler air
coming in
(little wind)

The same thing happens when the air is heated by sunshine. Of course, if all the air were heated evenly, it would all try to go up at once. But then there would be nothing to replace it, so it wouldn't move at all. But it hardly ever happens that the air is heated evenly by sunshine.

Most often, the air in one place stays cooler. Maybe one place is hidden by clouds, or maybe one place is over some cold ocean water. Then the air that is heated by sunshine rises, and air from the cooler place comes in to replace it. When we feel the air coming in, we call it wind.

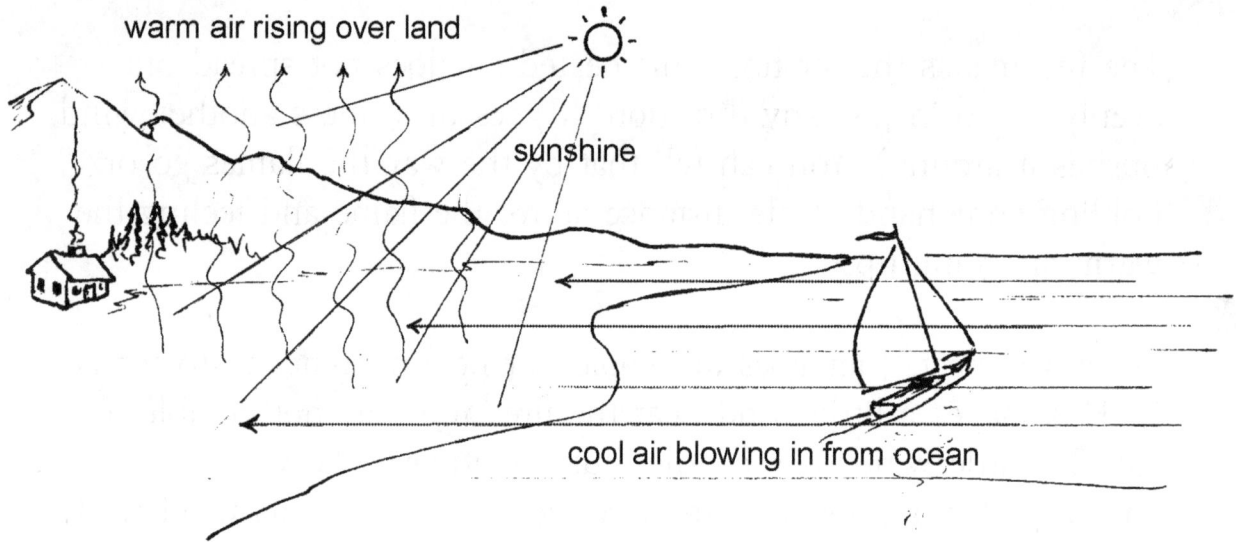

warm air rising over land

sunshine

cool air blowing in from ocean

LET'S DO THIS!
Make Some Wind

To do this activity, you will need

- heavy-duty electric hair dryer
- very lightweight plastic bag. The kind that is put over clean clothing at the dry cleaner is best.

Steps

1. Carefully fold over the long open end of the bag and tape or glue it closed. Close off the other end but leave enough space so the end of the hair dryer can go in and the extra air can come back out. The hanger opening on a dry-cleaning bag is about right.

2. Fill the bag with hot air from the hair dryer.[1] Try doing this by squeezing the bag opening around the hair dryer nozzle with your hand, but leaving a few inches open so that the extra air can come back out.

3. When the bag is full of hot air, it should start to lift up. (The air in the bag must get quite hot for this to work. It also helps if the air in the room is cool.)

4. When the bag starts to lift up, turn off the hair dryer and let go of the bag. Watch what happens.

5. Write what happened, and tell how this helps show how sunshine makes wind.

---

1 Most hair dryers turn themselves off automatically when they get too hot inside. If this happens, turn off the switch and let the hair dryer cool for several minutes before you use it again.

LET'S DO THIS!

Study the Wind

To do this activity, you will need

- your Weather Record sheet
- compass (if needed)

Steps

Do this activity when you go outside to measure the temperature in the morning and afternoon each day.

1. Decide if the wind speed is calm, breezy or windy. If it's windy, you can say if it's light, medium or strong wind. Write this on your Weather Record sheet.

2. Decide which direction the wind is going, and then write the direction of the wind on your sheet. If you need to, use a compass to tell the direction. Remember, wind direction is always named for where the wind comes from. (Don't stand too close to a building—that can make it hard to tell which way the wind is really coming from.)

3. Look at the weather, and decide if it is cloudy, rainy, or clear and sunny. Write this on your sheet.

4. Continue writing each of these things on your record sheet every day when you do your weather checks. This part of your Weather Record might look something like this when you are done:

Day No.	Date AM/PM		Air Temp.	Wind Type	Wind Direction	Weather Types	Cloud Types	Rain Meas.	Storm Types	Notes
1	Date	AM		calm	none	sunny				
		PM		breezy	east	cloudy				
2	Date	AM		breezy	east	cloudy				
		PM		windy	east	rain				
3	Date	AM		windy	east	rain				
		PM		light	east	cloudy				
4	Date	AM		calm	none	sunny				
		PM		light	west	sunny				
5	Date	AM		breezy	west	clouds				
		PM		calm	none	sunny				
6	Date	AM		calm	none	sunny				
		PM		breezy	west	sunny				
7	Date	AM		light	east	cloudy				
		PM		medium	east	rain				

5. The first time you do this, show your Weather Record sheet to another person.

Chapter 6

More About Wind

When there is less air in one place than in other places, air tends to rush in to fill up the first place. This is how winds occur.

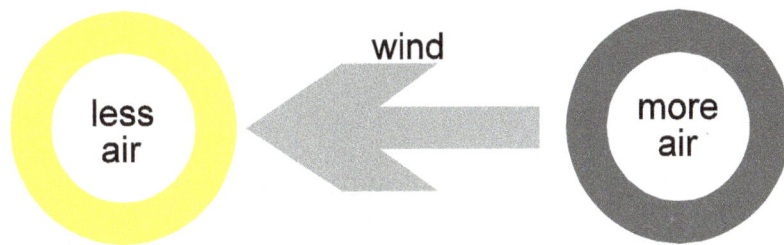

How does it happen that one place might have less air than other places?

As you read earlier, one of the main ways this happens is by warm air rising. If the air in one spot heats up more than the air in other places nearby, the air in that spot rises. That leaves not so much air in the spot, and the air from surrounding places tends to "blow" in to fill the spot back up. This is what we usually call wind.

warm air rising

surrounding air blowing in

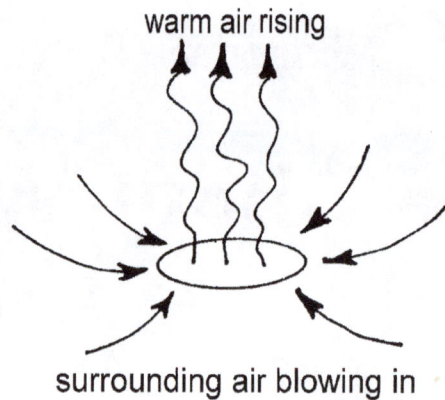

So winds are usually caused by warm air rising, and cooler air rushing in to take its place. Winds come in all sizes. There are little winds and there are big winds.

LITTLE WINDS

Sometimes you feel a little puff of wind, or you see the branches of a tree move for a few seconds. These little winds are caused by little differences in the temperature of the air, and they come and go quickly.

Maybe there is some cool air in the shade under a tree, but the sun is heating the air in a meadow nearby. Then the air in the meadow rises, and suddenly the air under the trees swirls out into the meadow, making it cooler there again.

So the air in the meadow stops rising, and the little puff of wind goes away.

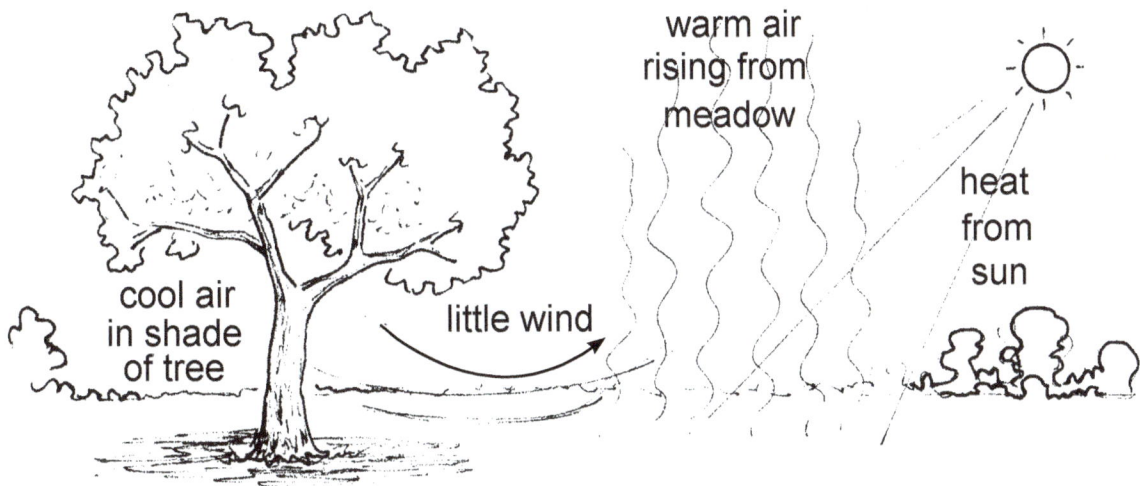

Sunshine often causes wind by warming the air. But the air doesn't get warmed very much just by sunshine passing through it. Otherwise the air would take most of the sun's heat, and there wouldn't be much left to make you feel warm when you stand in the sunshine. Actually the air is heated mostly by touching things that the sun heats up, like the ground or other objects.

MORNING AND EVENING BREEZES

There are winds that usually happen in the morning and the evening, especially in places where there is land with water nearby. These winds are bigger than the little meadow breezes. Here is how they happen:

The water takes the heat from the sun and holds it, but the land gives most of its heat back to the air. So in the morning when the sun comes up, the air over the water stays fairly cool, while the air over the land warms up from the sunshine.

When the air over the land starts to rise, the cooler air over the water blows in to replace it. This wind is called a **morning breeze**, because it only lasts until the air over the water gets mixed up with air from the land and isn't so much cooler any more.

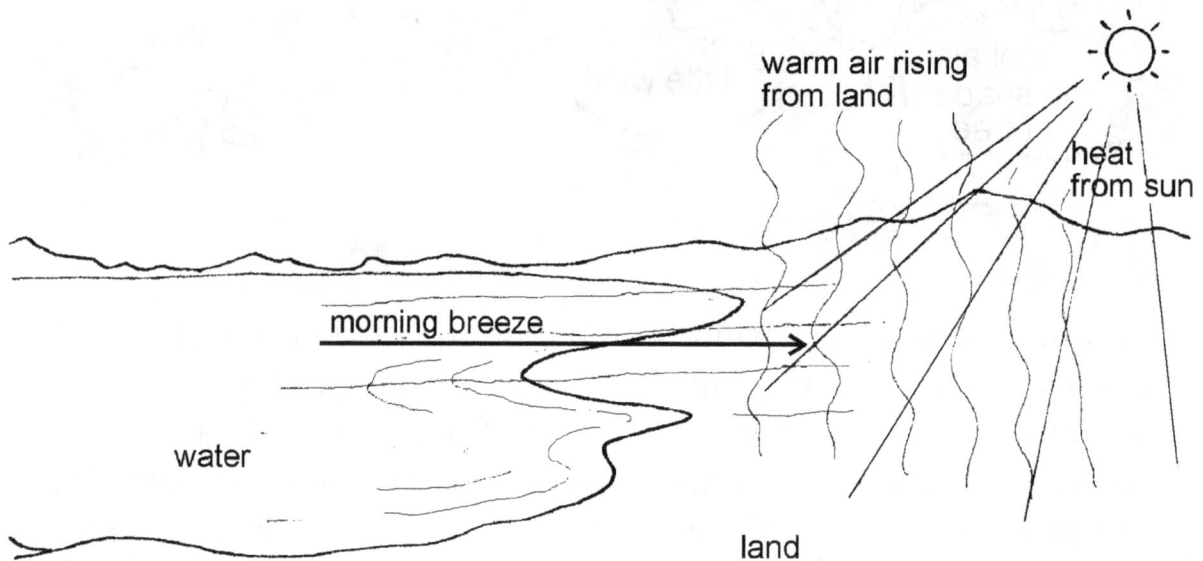

In the evening when the sun goes down, the land gives up all the heat it got from the sunshine and cools off quickly. But the water stays warmer because it loses its heat more slowly. So quite often the land becomes cooler than the water after sundown. Then it is the air over the water that starts to rise, and the air from the land blows toward the water to replace it. This is the **evening breeze**.

warmer air rising over water

cool night air
over land

water

evening breeze

land

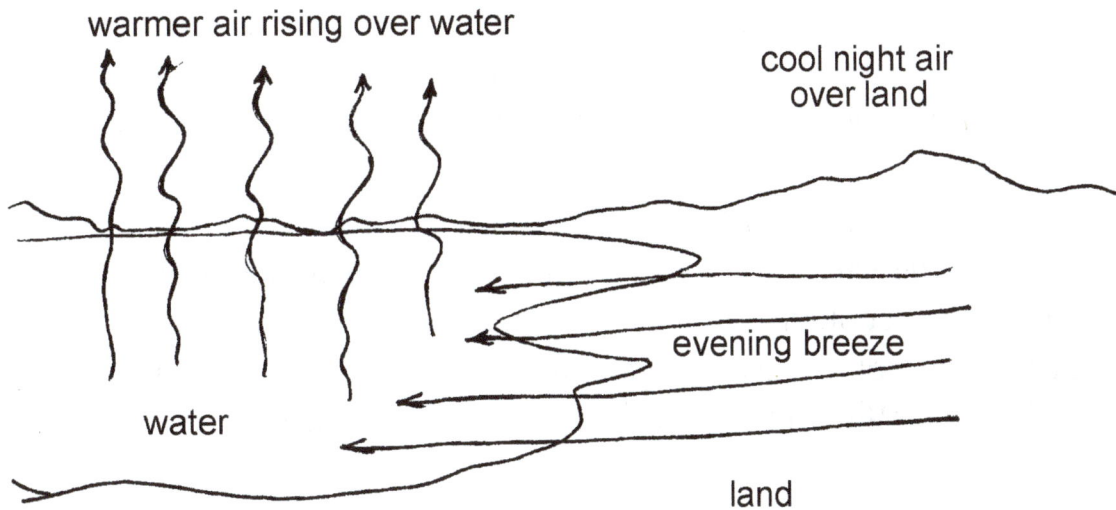

On the seashore, where there is a lot of cold water to keep the air cool, a gentle wind from the water to the land can keep going all day long. That wind is often called a **sea breeze**.

WHAT HAPPENS AFTER THE AIR RISES?

You probably wonder what happens to the air that goes up. It must come down again somewhere, but where, and why?

To answer that, we need to notice something more about air. We have already noticed that air goes up when it gets hot, and cooler air comes in to replace it. To figure out why this is, think about a hot air balloon, the big colorful kind that carries people up in the air in a big basket. The only way a balloon like that can go up is if the balloon is lighter than air. The only thing that can make the balloon lighter than air is if the hot air inside the balloon is lighter than the air around it. So that is why hot air goes up. It is because hot air is lighter than cooler air.

We also know that hot things tend to cool off after a while. When the air heated by sunshine rises up high, it gives up its extra heat to the air around it. Some of the heat even goes out into space.

Actually that is a good thing. If all the heat from the sunshine stayed on the earth, the earth would get hotter and hotter and we would all be cooked! But what happens instead is that when the ground gets hot, it heats the air above it, and when the air gets hot, it rises. When the hot air rises high enough, it gives off some of its heat to space.

The earth gives off exactly as much heat to space this way as it receives from the sun in the first place, so instead of getting hotter, or cooling off too much, it stays about the same all the time.

Some people might think this is a lucky accident, but it is not. If the air gets hotter, it gives off more heat to space and cools down. If it gets cooler, it gives off less heat to space and warms up. That's why it works out evenly and stays about the same all the time.

After the air higher up loses its extra heat to space and becomes cooler, it can't rise any more. It starts to go down instead, and is replaced by heated air rising from someplace else.

heat going into space

high moving air

cool air
falling

warm air
rising

wind near the ground

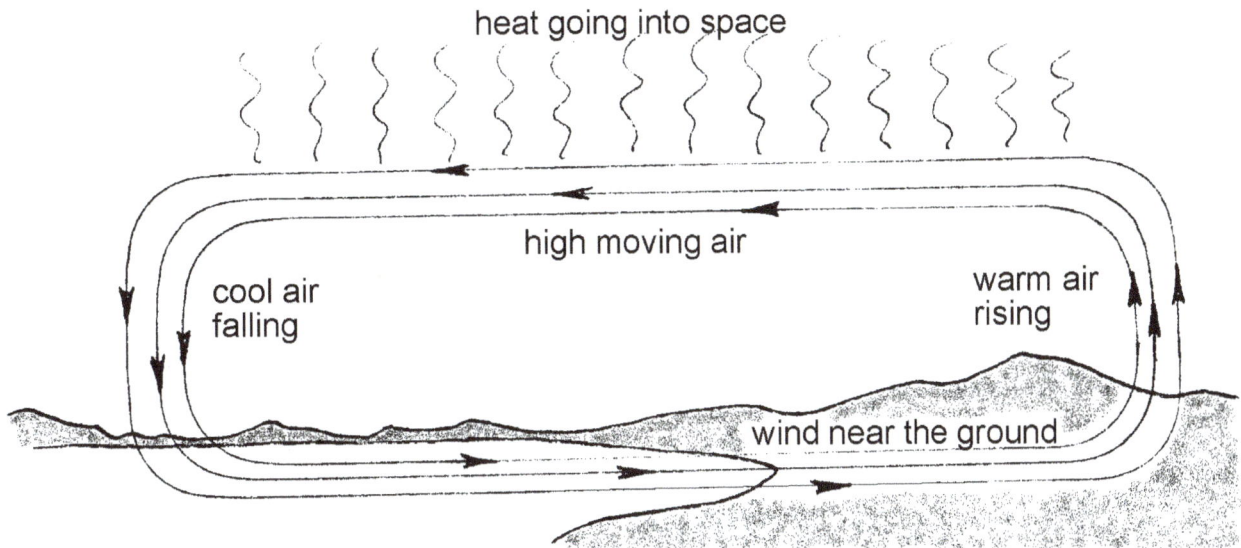

While the hot air is rising and the cool air is falling, you can see that there has to be air going sideways. The sideways moving air along the ground is what we feel as wind. But the sideways moving air higher up is another wind. This wind completes a circle of air movement.

Now you can see that the sunshine warming the earth causes the air to move in big circles, and the winds we feel are just part of this movement of air.

Chapter 7

Storms

We talked about little meadow breezes, and about morning and evening breezes, but there are bigger winds than these.

A **storm** is a strong wind usually with heavy rain or snow. It is usually cold and cloudy and sometimes there is thunder and lightning.

Storms usually last between one and three days. After that, the weather usually changes to another type, such as fair and sunny. Sometimes, however, two or more storms can follow each other, so that one will barely stop before another one begins.

When the winds of a storm don't have a lot of rain, it is called a **windstorm**.

If a storm brings lots of snow it is called a **snowstorm**. If it is a big enough snowstorm with very strong winds, it is called a **blizzard**.

A storm that brings rain is called a **rainstorm**. If a rainstorm is too heavy or lasts too long, the water may be too much for lakes and rivers to hold. Then the water may go places where it doesn't usually go. When there is lots of water where there usually is no water, it is called a **flood**.

Storms are interesting because they are a moving and changing type of weather. Not all storms bring trouble. In fact, most storms are good because they bring us fresh water in the form of rain or snow.

Storms bring us the water we need to grow crops, to fill the lakes and rivers, to drink and bathe and cook with. We need the water that storms bring to work and live well.

LET'S DO THIS!
Recording Storms

To do this activity, you will need

- your Weather Record sheet

Steps

1. Look over your Weather Record so far, and remember if you had a storm on any of those days.

2. If you did, try to remember the motion of trees, clouds, rain, wind, and everything else that you can. Decide what kind of storm it was and write that down on your Weather Record for that day.

3. Do the same for any more storms that happen while you are keeping weather records.

Chapter 8

Winds Up High

The winds high up can be very big winds. When the winds are so high, they can be above the land and the water and even above the tallest mountains. There is nothing to get in their way and slow them down.

These big winds swirl and blow all around the world in huge streams. They are driven by air that is rising or falling over whole oceans or continents, from parts of the planet that are in sunlight and from parts where it is night. They rise from parts of the planet that are hot, like the tropics, and they go down at parts where it is cold, like the poles.

Sometimes on big weather maps you see pictures of these winds that go zooming around Earth. One of these high fast winds is called the **jet stream**. The winds in the jet stream go very fast, up to 125 miles an hour!

= jet stream

Imagine if you were in an airplane and you flew along with the jet stream. You could get where you were going much faster. Big airliners actually do this and it speeds up travel. Of course it wouldn't be very smart to fly in the jet stream going the other way, so the airliners don't do that.

The jet stream and other big winds that blow high up are important to our weather, because they have a big effect on what the winds near the ground will do. The jet stream can bring cold air down from the Arctic, or warm air up from the tropics, and mix it with the air in the area in between to make that weather cooler or warmer.

BIG STORMS

Winds that are high up will sometimes form big swirling circles, called **cyclones**. You can often see cyclones in the pictures taken by weather satellites. They look something like the way water does when it goes swirling down a drain.

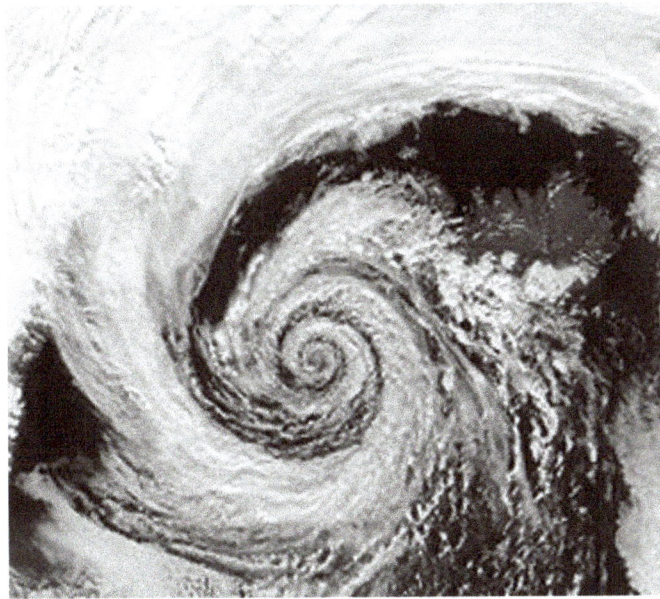

Sometimes these big winds reach all the way to the ground, and bring huge storms. **Hurricanes** are large cyclones that get wound up very tight and have very fast winds in them, from high up right down to the ground. When a hurricane passes over land, it usually tears things up, including blowing down trees and damaging houses.

Another wind that is very strong and dangerous but not so big is a tornado. **Tornadoes** are kind of like tiny hurricanes. They usually are not nearly as wide as hurricanes and do not last very long. But they get wound up so tight that the winds in the center are strong enough to tear the roofs off of houses and toss cars around. A tornado might be just about as wide as a soccer field or even smaller, while a hurricane is miles across.

Winds are a very important part of weather, and they come in all shapes and sizes. But they are all driven the same way—by the circling of air as it gets heated by the sun shining on the earth and cooled by letting the heat go off into space.

LET'S DO THIS!
Show How a Tornado Swirls

To do this activity, you will need

- two large plastic soda bottles
- tape
- water

Steps

1. Fill one of the soda bottles a little more than half full of water.

2. Put the other bottle upside down on top of the first one, neck to neck, and tape them together so they won't come apart.

3. Turn the bottles over so the water can run from the first bottle down into the second one.

4. Swirl the bottles a little bit to get the water to spin like a tornado as it goes down. Keep trying it until you can make this happen.

5. Notice that as the water swirls down, the air in the bottom gets sucked up into the top bottle.

Chapter 9

Clouds

Have you ever wondered what clouds are?

Some clouds are round and puffy, like huge balls of cotton.

Others are small and thin and look like feathers.

Still others are thick and dark and come with storms.

All **clouds** are the same in one way. They are all made of water droplets.

If clouds are made of water, then why don't they fall to the ground?

The answer to this question is that they do fall! But they fall so slowly that they hardly ever hit the ground. Usually the air that is under them is pushing them up as fast as they fall down.

Think of a balloon. If you let go of a balloon up in the air, it would slowly fall to the ground. But if you blew air up under the balloon, you could keep it from falling. The air under clouds acts like your breath on the balloon and keeps the clouds from falling. Sometimes the air under a cloud is moving up so fast that the cloud actually rises.

Air moving up under clouds keeps them from falling.

The air that moves up under clouds does not have to move very fast, because the clouds are falling very slowly. They fall slowly because the water droplets they are made of are so tiny.

Things that are very small fall through the air slowly because the air slows them down. The droplets of a cloud are usually too small to see, but if you could make them much bigger, they would look something like this picture:

Part of a cloud made much bigger to show the tiny water droplets.

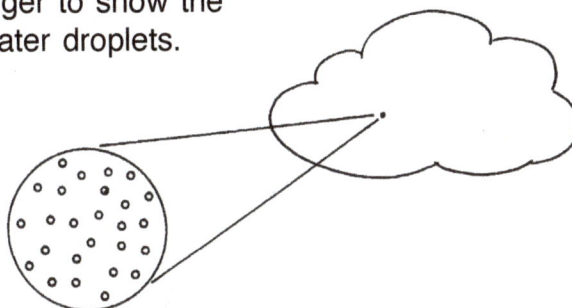

Although you can't see each water droplet in a cloud, you can see all the droplets together. And that's what a **cloud** is—a lot of water droplets together in the air.

So now we know that clouds are made up of water droplets. But even regular air has water in it. We'll find out more about this later in the book. But for now, just know that clouds form when warm air with water in it hits cold air.

Clouds can be different colors. White clouds are clouds that have the sun shining off of them.

Gray clouds are clouds that are hiding the sun. When clouds are very dark, they are usually very thick. They are dark because they don't let much sunlight through them.

Clouds can be red or pink or orange when the sun is going down or coming up and shines pink or orange light on them from the bottom.

Sometimes clouds will bring rain, and sometimes they won't. There are some things that will help you tell if the clouds will bring rain or not.

If the clouds are white and puffy, and there is a lot of blue in the sky, then these clouds will probably not rain. We sometimes call these white puffy clouds **fair weather clouds.**

If the sky is all cloudy and dark gray, you had better wear a raincoat or carry an umbrella, because it will probably rain that day. We usually call these dark gray clouds **rain clouds** or **storm clouds**.

Clouds can be any different size or shape. They can cover the whole sky or be just in one little spot. Sometimes clouds have shapes that can look like trees or animals or other things. Clouds can be fun to watch, and they are an important part of the weather too.

LET'S DO THIS!
Make a Cloud

To do this activity, you will need

- a freezer

Steps

1. Slowly open the freezer door.

2. Blow your breath inside the freezer with your mouth wide open, and notice the small cloud that forms inside the freezer. This cloud is made of water droplets that formed when the water that is in your warm breath hit the cold air in the freezer. Clouds outside also form when warm air with water in it hits cold air.

3. Tell another person what happened when you did this activity, and explain what clouds are made of.

LET'S DO THIS!
Study the Clouds

To do this activity, you will need

- your Weather Record sheet

Steps

Do this activity when you go outside to do your weather check in the morning and afternoon each day.

1. Look at the sky and notice what kind of clouds you can see.

2. Write down what kind of clouds they are in the "Cloud Types" column of your Weather Record. You might say whether they are puffy or feathery, white or gray, high or low, light or heavy. For example, there might be "high, white, feathery" clouds, or "low, dark, heavy" clouds.

3. Also write down if you think the clouds will bring rain soon or not.

4. Continue writing these things on your record sheet every day when you do your weather checks.

Chapter 10

Rain

When heavy dark clouds fill the sky, we usually expect to get some rain, because the water in the clouds is likely to fall. But the water from the clouds can come down in many different forms.

Sometimes we get a very light rain, just a **sprinkle**.

Other times we get a very heavy rain, a real **downpour**.

Sometimes the rain is so light and fine, it is hard to tell if it is falling at all. It is just a **mist** that may be blown up or down by little gusts of wind.

Sometimes we go outside in the morning, and the ground is damp even though there has been no rain at all. The dampness has settled out of the air onto the ground and onto other things as the air cooled off overnight. We call this morning dampness **dew**.

When the air is cold enough, the water in the air changes into ice. It freezes into tiny ice crystals that may grow to be quite big as they fall and more water freezes onto them. These crystals are called **snowflakes**.

If the air is cold, but it is not quite cold enough for snow, we may get **sleet**. Sleet is rain that is so cold that some of it turns to ice as it falls. Another name for sleet is freezing rain. It can coat trees and sidewalks with ice. When the sun comes out after an ice storm, everything shines and it can be quite beautiful. But it can also be dangerous, because it is hard to walk on icy sidewalks!

Another kind of ice storm is **hail**. This happens when rain starts falling and freezes into round balls of ice on the way down. These are called hailstones. Hailstones are usually small, like raindrops, but if more and more water freezes onto these balls of ice, they can get as big as golf balls. Sometimes there are even hailstones that get as big as baseballs! Big hailstones can do damage, sometimes breaking windows and denting the tops of cars, and ruining farmers' crops.

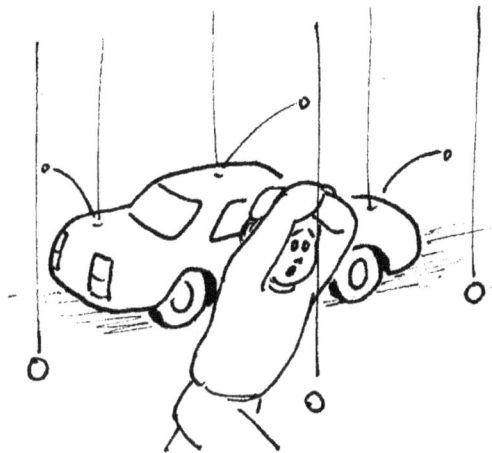

Water can come down in many forms. Some forms can be beautiful, and some forms can be dangerous. Some forms can be both beautiful and dangerous. But all forms bring us fresh clean water. And sometimes rain brings us an extra prize—a rainbow!

Chapter 11

Evaporation and Condensation

Water in the weather is always changing form. In some places in the world water is freezing. In other places, it is **evaporating**, which means going from liquid water up into the air.

In other places, water is **condensing**, which just means going from the air back into liquid, usually forming tiny droplets.

So how does this work? Let's look at evaporation and condensation more closely.

EVAPORATION

When water evaporates, it changes from liquid to vapor. **Water vapor** is very tiny bits of water that have gone into the air and become invisible. You can't see, smell or taste water vapor.

Water can evaporate at any temperature, but it usually evaporates faster when the water and air are warmer.

Have you ever gotten out of a pool on a hot day and felt cold? Maybe you used a towel to dry off and felt warmer.

When water evaporates, it absorbs (takes in) heat from any object it is touching. This causes the object to get cooler. When you were wet from the pool, the water on your body was evaporating and absorbing heat from your skin. As you dried off, there was less water to absorb your heat and you felt warmer.

Your body uses this same process to cool you on a hot day. When you sweat, your body uses the sweat to absorb some of your body's heat and cool you off.

When water evaporates, it seems to disappear. It turns to vapor, which is invisible.

CONDENSATION

When water vapor cools, the tiny invisible bits of water come together and change back into liquid. We say the vapor condenses.

When you breathe on a window glass, the water vapor in the air turns into tiny droplets that show up as mist on the glass. This is because the glass is usually cooler than your breath. When the water vapor in your warm breath hits the cool glass, it condenses.

The same thing happens when a glass of cold liquid is put in a warmer room. As the warmer water vapor in the air touches the cold glass, it condenses into water droplets.

TEMPERATURE

So what is it that causes water to change form? Temperature!

Heat makes ice melt and water evaporate. Cold makes water freeze and vapor condense.

LET'S DO THIS!
Forms of Water

To do this activity, you will need

- glass
- water
- ice cubes

Steps

1. Blow on a cool window or mirror. Do you see a mist on the glass? What does this show about your breath and water vapor?

2. Put ice cubes in a glass of water, and set it in a warm room.

3. Watch for water drops to begin to form on the outside of the glass. It may take several minutes.

4. Let the glass sit undisturbed for an hour and then go back and look at it again. What does it look like now?

5. Tell (or write up for) someone what happened with the glass of ice water, and what it tells you about how much water vapor is in the air.

Chapter 12

Water on Earth

Water on Earth is always evaporating or condensing.

When it is warm and sunny, more evaporation than condensation occurs.

When it is cooler, cloudy and rainy, more condensation than evaporation occurs.

THE WATER CYCLE

In a **cycle**, things that are related in some way happen over and over again in the same order. Day and night are a cycle. The seasons are a cycle. We have spring, summer, fall and winter—over and over again, always in the same order.

On Earth, water goes through a cycle of evaporation and condensation.

It starts as liquid on the earth's surface. This could be an ocean, a lake, or something as small as a puddle on the sidewalk.

As the sun shines on the water, it warms up and some of it evaporates, changing from liquid to water vapor.

The water vapor rises into the air, higher and higher, until it is miles above the surface of Earth.

Because the air above the earth is colder, the water vapor cools as it rises. When it is cool enough, it condenses into small liquid drops of water that form clouds.

When the clouds get heavy enough with water drops, the water falls as rain (or snow that eventually melts). It's liquid again!

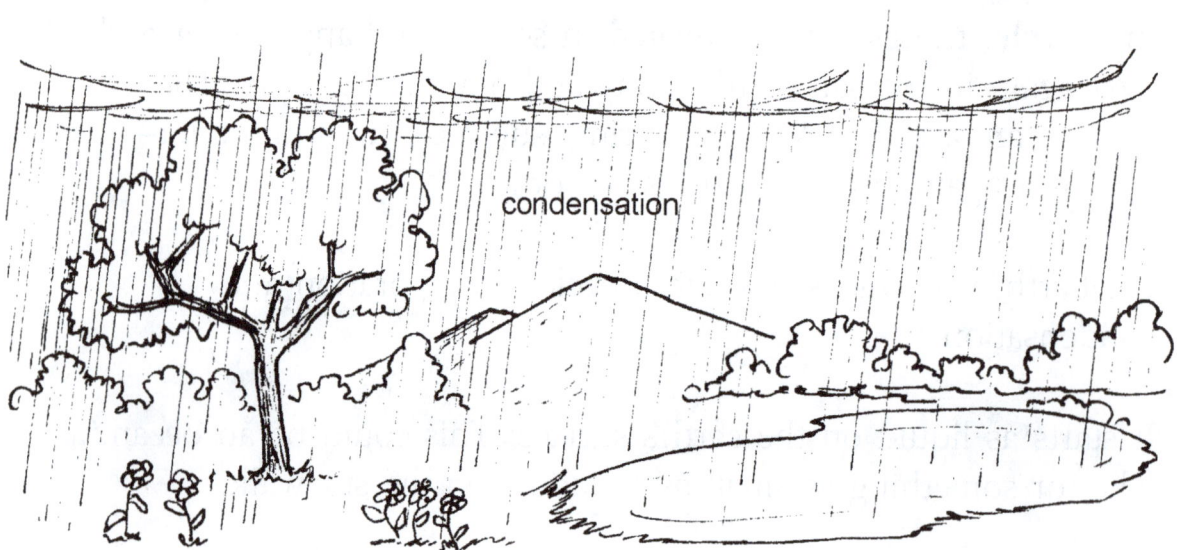

This is the **water cycle**, and it's happening everywhere in the world, all the time.

WATER'S JOURNEY

The journey of water involves oceans, streams and rivers, clouds, rain and snow. Now that you know about the water cycle, let's follow one drop of water on its journey.

Our water drop starts in the ocean. The sun warms our drop until it becomes water vapor in the air.

As it rises above the earth, it gets cooler and cooler until it condenses back into liquid and becomes a cloud. The cloud gets heavier and heavier as more water drops collect. Let's say that the air is so cold that the water drops freeze. Our water drop now falls to the ground as a snowflake.

Our snowflake stays on the ground until the sun melts it back into water. It joins the rest of the melted snow, and flows into a tiny stream. It is carried along until the stream meets a river.

Our water drop now travels along with the river until it gets back to where it started--the ocean!

Of course, our water drop doesn't have to start or end in the ocean. Maybe it evaporates from a puddle. Or even from the wet earth. Have you ever seen fog rising from cool, wet earth when the warm sun shines on it? That is liquid water on its way to becoming water vapor.

There is no start or end to the journey of water. Whether or not snow is involved, water is always on a journey. And wherever on Earth that journey is taking place, the water cycle is repeating over and over again. This is nature's way of recycling water!

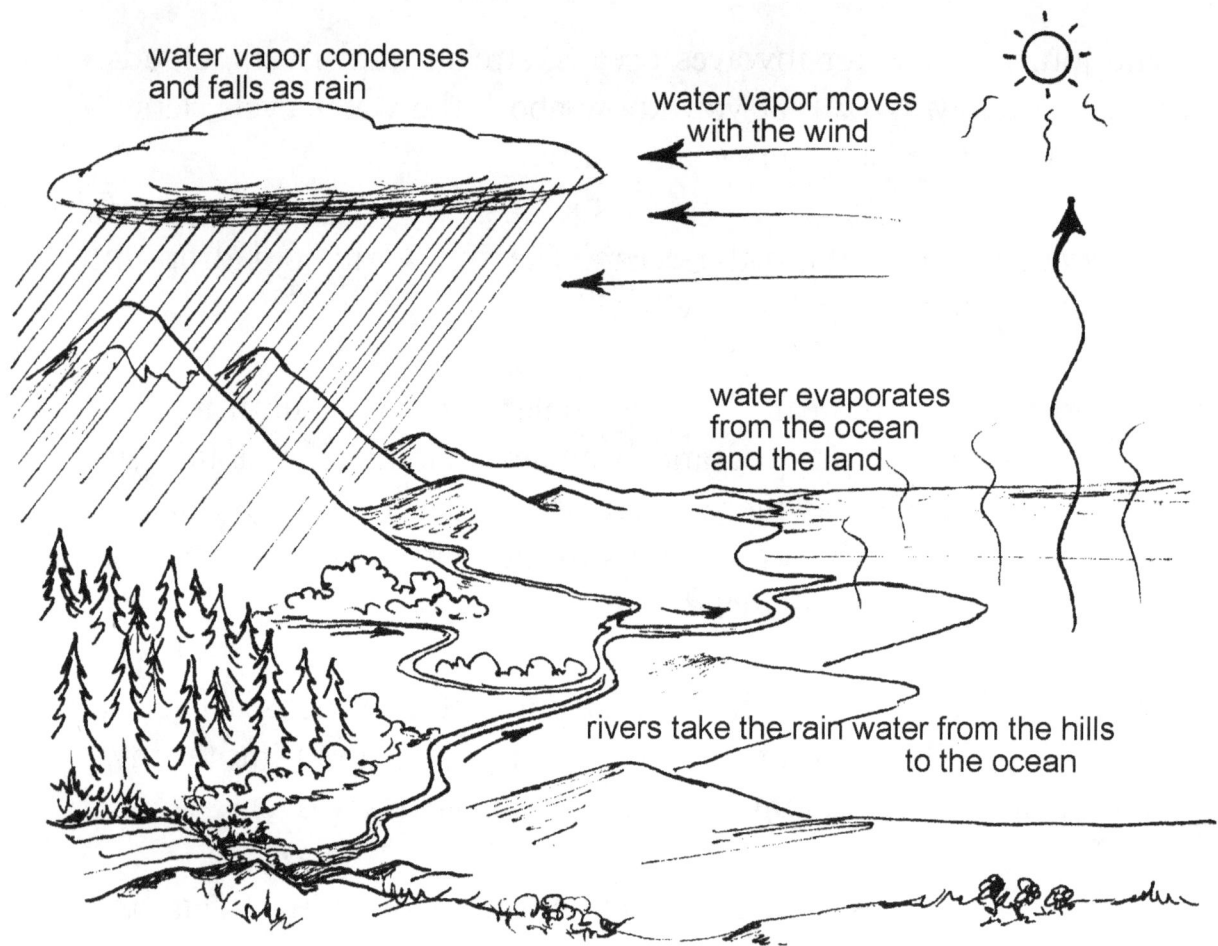

water vapor condenses
and falls as rain

water vapor moves
with the wind

water evaporates
from the ocean
and the land

rivers take the rain water from the hills
to the ocean

LET'S DO THIS!
The Water Cycle

To do this activity, you will need

- two flat pans
- plate
- hot plate or stove burner
- several ice cubes

Steps

1. Put about half an inch of water in the bottom of one pan.

2. Place this pan on a hot plate or burner. Bring the water to a boil.

3. Put several ice cubes in another pan and hold it above the pan on the burner, tilting one corner down slightly. Keep your hands away from the steam from the boiling water—it's hot!

4. At the same time, hold the plate on a slant between the low end of the pan with ice in it and the pan on the burner.

5. What do you see happening? How do you think this relates to the water cycle on Earth? Tell (or write up for) someone else your answers to these questions.

The pans and plate should look something like this:

LET'S DO THIS!
Measure Rain

To do this activity, you will need

- Rain gauge (any small can with a flat bottom, straight sides and open top to collect rain water may be used, along with a measuring stick).
- your Weather Record sheet

Steps

Do this activity when you go outside to do your weather check in the morning and afternoon each day.

1. Set up your rain gauge outside in a flat, open place.

2. Check the rain gauge every day when you do your weather checks. If you are using a can for your rain gauge, use a small measuring stick to see how deep the water is.

3. Write down on your Weather Record how much rain you measure, then empty the rain gauge for the next day. (If there is no rain, write "no rain.")

4. Continue writing the rain measurement two times every day when you do your weather checks.

Chapter 13

Lightning and Thunder

Lightning is a crooked streak of very bright light that usually goes from the clouds to the ground or the ground to the clouds. Sometimes it just streaks between clouds. Sometimes the streak has many branches. Sometimes the crooked streak cannot be seen and the lightning just looks like a flash of very bright light.

Lightning happens during big storms. It is caused by electricity flowing between clouds and the ground or between clouds. These storms are called lightning storms, or sometimes electrical storms.

There may be many lightning flashes during such a storm. Each streak of lightning happens very fast, usually in less than a second. During the streak it may blink several times. Lightning may be so bright that it makes night look like day for a second.

Some parts of the world have lightning often, and some parts don't.

TELLING HOW FAR AWAY LIGHTNING IS

Thunder is a rumbling sound that goes along with lightning. It is the sound that air makes when lightning cuts through it. Usually it starts with a loud *boom* or *crack*. Thunder can sound a lot like a jet airplane flying close by.

You can always tell how close lightning is by the thunder. You always hear the thunder after the lightning flash because the sound takes longer to get to you than the light does. If you hear thunder right after you see lightning, then you know that the lightning is close by.

You can tell how far away the lightning is by counting the number of seconds between the flash and when you hear the first boom of the thunder. To count the seconds, say "thousand and 1, thousand and 2, thousand and 3," and so on. Counting that way, each number takes about a second to say.

If there are only one or two seconds between the flash and the thunder, then the lightning is very close. If there are 5 seconds between the flash and the thunder, then the lightning is about a mile away. If there are 10 seconds between the two, the lightning is about 2 miles away. If you count 15 seconds, then the lightning is about 3 miles away. For every 5 seconds between the flash of lightning and the first sound of the thunder that goes with it, the lightning is about one more mile away.

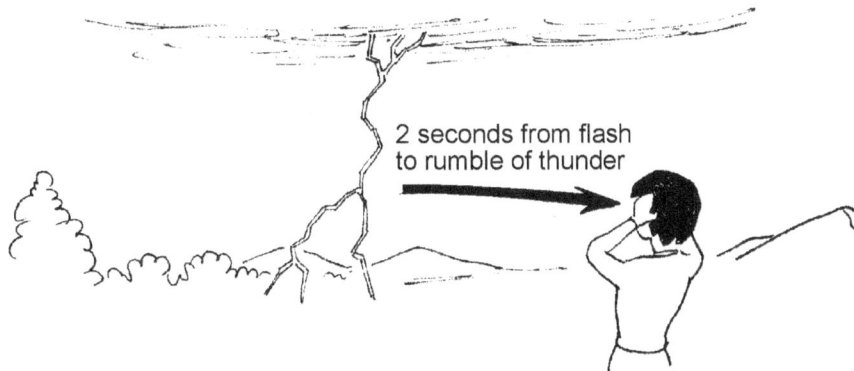

2 seconds from flash to rumble of thunder

Lightning here is close by.

5 seconds from flash to rumble of thunder

Lightning here is about one mile away.

15 seconds from flash
to rumble of thunder

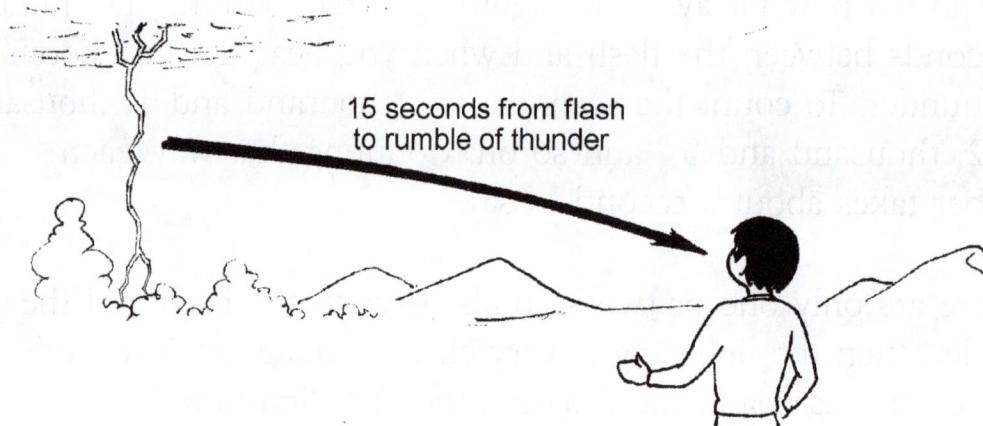

Lightning here is about three miles away.

LIGHTNING STRIKES

Lightning does not always strike the ground, but when it does it can cause damage to whatever it strikes. This is because the electricity flowing in lightning makes things it touches very hot. It is so hot that it can easily start fires where it strikes.

It can also harm people and animals, and damage trees and houses.

Lightning usually strikes the tallest thing around. This may be a tree or a telephone pole or the top of a hill. But it could be you, if you are standing where you are the tallest thing around!

When people get struck by lightning, they are usually injured, or sometimes even killed. But one man was hit by lightning three different times and survived! If you are outside, and lightning is nearby (less than 3 second away), the safest thing to do is to get inside a building, or car with the windows up, quickly.

If a building or car are not close enough, stay away from hills and other high points, including isolated trees. If in a forest, stay within a small group of trees. If you have to stand near a tree, stand as far away as possible.

Near a tree is the *second* worst place to be in a lightning storm. The worst place of all is in the open. If you are the highest thing around (for example, if you are standing in the middle of an open field), you should find the nearest low area, and crouch down like a ball with your head tucked in so you are as low as possible but touching the ground as little as possible. Never lie down on the ground, even if you are in an open space, as that makes you a bigger target for lightning.

If you are on a lake, be sure to get off the lake and out of the water when you hear thunder or see lightning. Remember, lightning strikes the highest thing around. If you are on a lake, you might be the highest thing.

Lightning is interesting and fun to watch. It is a natural fireworks display. Just make sure you are in a safe place while you watch it.

LET'S DO THIS!
Lightning Safety

Steps

1. Go outside and find three places where it would not be safe to stand if lightning were near.

2. Find three places that would be safe to be if lightning were near.

3. Decide where the safest place would be if lightning were near.

4. Pretend you are in a field where you are the tallest thing, and lightning is near. What would you do if you couldn't quickly get inside?

5. Tell (or write up for) someone:

   a) about all the places you found and why they are safe or not safe.

   b) which place you decided was safest and why you picked that one.

   c) what you would do if you were the tallest thing in an open field.

LET'S DO THIS!
Lightning Distance

Steps

1. Find how far away the lightning is for each of the times listed below. The column on the left tells the time between a lightning flash and the first sound of thunder. The column on the right tells how far away the lightning is.

   Copy the first column on a piece of paper, then match the times with the correct distances in the second column and write in the distances.

Time Between Lightning and Thunder	Lightning is This Far Away:
5 seconds	2 miles away
10 seconds	very close
15 seconds	1 mile away
1 second	about 2 miles away
6 seconds	3 miles away
9 seconds	about 1 mile away

2. Show your work to another person.

3. Get another person to be your partner. Have your partner say "FLASH!" and then you count the seconds ("thousand and 1, thousand and 2, thousand and 3," and so on) until your partner says "BOOM!" Then you tell how far away the lightning is. Repeat with different distances until you can get the distances easily.

4. If you are lucky enough to have a lightning storm while you are doing the rest of this book, count the seconds and try to tell how far away the lightning is. Do this several times, and notice if the lightning is getting closer or moving away. Decide how close the lightning storm got to where you were.

Chapter 14

Changing Weather

The weather is always changing. It is never exactly the same on any two days, but sometimes it's similar for several days in a row. We can say that we have a certain type of weather during those days.

There are several different common types of weather.

FAIR WEATHER

When the sky is clear and the weather is generally nice to be in, it is called **fair weather**. Fair weather may last several days, or it may last weeks or months. Fair weather may be hot or cool, windy or calm. Whatever else it is, fair weather is sunny and mostly clear, with never more than a few little white clouds in the sky.

Fair weather

CLOUDY WEATHER

Cloudy weather is weather where there are clouds in the sky. If some of the sky is cloudy and some is clear, this type of weather is called **partly cloudy**.

Partly cloudy

When all of the sky is covered with clouds, the type of weather is called **overcast**. You cannot see the sun when the weather is overcast.

overcast

It doesn't matter if the wind is blowing or how hot it is. Partly cloudy and overcast weather depend only on clouds. Cloudy weather can last for several days, but rarely lasts for more than a couple of weeks at a time.

FOG

When a cloud is near the ground, it is a special type of weather called **fog**. Fog is made of tiny droplets of water, just as clouds are. If you have ever been in fog, then you know what it is like to be inside a cloud. The difference between fog and clouds is just that fog is near the ground, and clouds are up in the air.

Fog is light gray in color and can be thick or thin. When it is thick, you cannot see very far in it. When it is thin, it makes things far away look hazy and blurry. Fog can be dangerous to drive a car in when it is thick, because it is not easy to see where you are going, or what is in the road in front of you.

Fog is usually thickest in the morning and at night, and thinnest during mid-day. Often fog will rise off the ground during mid-day to become overcast weather, and settle back down at night to become fog again.

Fog is light gray in color. It is thickest at night and in the morning.

STORMY WEATHER

Stormy weather is the type of weather that comes with storms. It is usually made up of cloudy, windy, and cold weather and always brings some form of rain. Lightning and thunder often come with stormy weather. Stormy weather usually only lasts for a few days.

OTHER TYPES OF WEATHER

There are other types of weather. There is hot weather when the air outside is hot, and cold weather when the air outside is cold. We have windy weather when the wind is blowing hard.

We can have more than one of these types of weather at the same time. We can have fair weather and hot weather at the same time, or it can be fair and cold. We can have fair and windy weather, or it can be fair and calm. It can be fair, hot and windy, or it can be overcast, windy and cold.

Sometimes part of the weather stays the same, but another part changes. We may have fair weather for a week, but on one day it may be calm and hot, and on the next day windy and cool.

Weather is made up of sunshine, temperature, wind, clouds, rain, and so on. There are many different ways that these go together to make up the weather every day. But no matter how the weather changes, it can be called one of these four main types: fair, cloudy, foggy or stormy.

LET'S DO THIS!

Types of Weather

To do this activity, you will need

- your Weather Record sheet

Steps

1. Take a short walk outside. Decide which of the four main types of weather (fair, cloudy, foggy or stormy) is going on outside right now. Also decide what other types of weather (hot or cold, windy or calm) are going on at the same time.

2. Write a paragraph describing the type of weather you had for your walk.

3. Now imagine that you took the same walk as before, but it was one of the other main types of weather.

4. Use your imagination to write a paragraph describing how that walk would have been different.

5. Write two more paragraphs describing imaginary walks in the other two main types of weather, so you have one paragraph for each of the four main types.

6. Look over your Weather Record. Notice the different types of weather you had.

7. Decide which of the four main types of weather you had each day, and write that down on your record sheet along with any other types of weather.

8. Show your paragraphs and your Weather Record to another person.

9. Continue noting the types of weather every day when you do your weather checks.

Chapter 15

Predicting the Weather

Predict means to tell what you think or know will happen in the future.

Many things go to make up the weather. Sunshine, temperature, wind, clouds and rain all are parts of weather. To be able to predict what the weather will be, you have to be able to figure out what all these things will do together.

Weather moves with the wind. Little winds bring little changes in the weather. Big winds bring big changes. It used to be hard to know much about the big winds, but now it is easier. There are weather satellites in orbit around Earth that send pictures of what the weather looks like from space. In addition to other things, the weather satellite pictures show the big winds by showing how the winds push clouds around.

People who study and predict the weather are called **meteorologists**. With all the information they gather about the different things that affect the weather, they can predict the weather about 5-10 days in advance.

Meteorologists make maps that show the patterns of the weather all over the country. You can see these maps on television news reports or online weather sites. If you study these maps, you can try to predict the weather from them too. For example, if a big wind is coming your way, and it is coming from a place that is having stormy weather, then you can expect the stormy weather to come your way too. If the wind coming your way is coming from a fair weather area, then you can expect some fair weather.

AIR PRESSURE

One of the things meteorologists know about that helps them predict the weather is **air pressure**. The air around us has weight, and it presses against everything it touches on Earth. That pressure, whether it is light or heavy, is air pressure. Air pressure changes with different kinds of weather.

You probably have had experience with air pressure when you blew up a balloon. By blowing air in a balloon, you make higher air pressure in the balloon, and this presses the balloon out and makes it bigger. When you release the air out of a balloon, the air pressure in the balloon goes down and the balloon is able to squeeze in and get smaller.

In weather, something like that happens when air rises. You can imagine that if air were rising away from a field, there wouldn't be quite as much air right above the field. So the air pressure above the field would be lower. This makes it possible for air around that area to blow in to fill it up.

When air is coming back down (pushing more air into the space), there is high air pressure.

So this is what makes the wind blow—air moving from a high pressure area to a low pressure area.

Knowing if there is high or low air pressure is important to predicting the weather. That is why weather maps often have a big letter **L** (for low) where the air is rising, and a big letter **H** (for high) where it is coming back down. When you look at one of these maps, you can figure that wind will be blowing away from the **H** and to the **L**, even if there are no wind arrows drawn on the map to show it.

WEATHER FRONTS

Another thing you will see on weather maps is thick lines with bumps or triangles on them. These lines show where there is a big change in the weather, such as from warm and rainy to cool and dry. The line is called a **front** because it shows the front of a weather change, where the change begins.

A line with triangles is a **cold front**, and the front moves in the direction the triangles point. A line with bumps is a **warm front**, and the front moves in the direction of the bumps. A line with triangles on one side and bumps on the other side is called a **stationary front**. This means it is not moving.

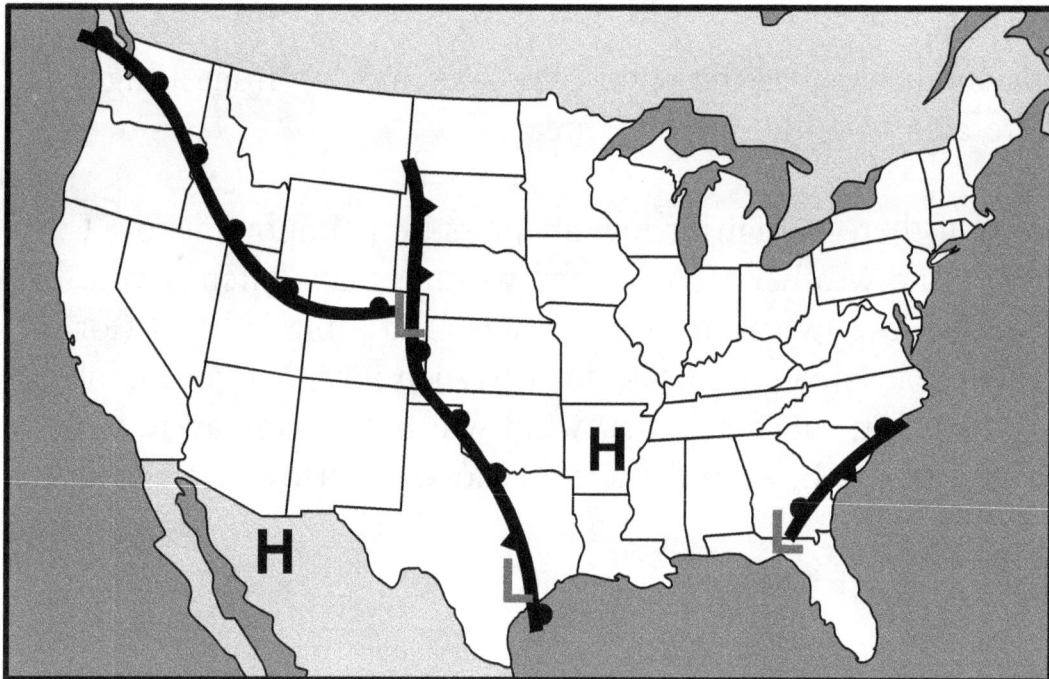

MAP 1

	cold front
	warm front
	stationary front

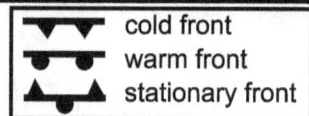

Remember, wind blows from high pressure to low pressure. It does not always blow the way a front is moving, the front just shows where the weather changes.

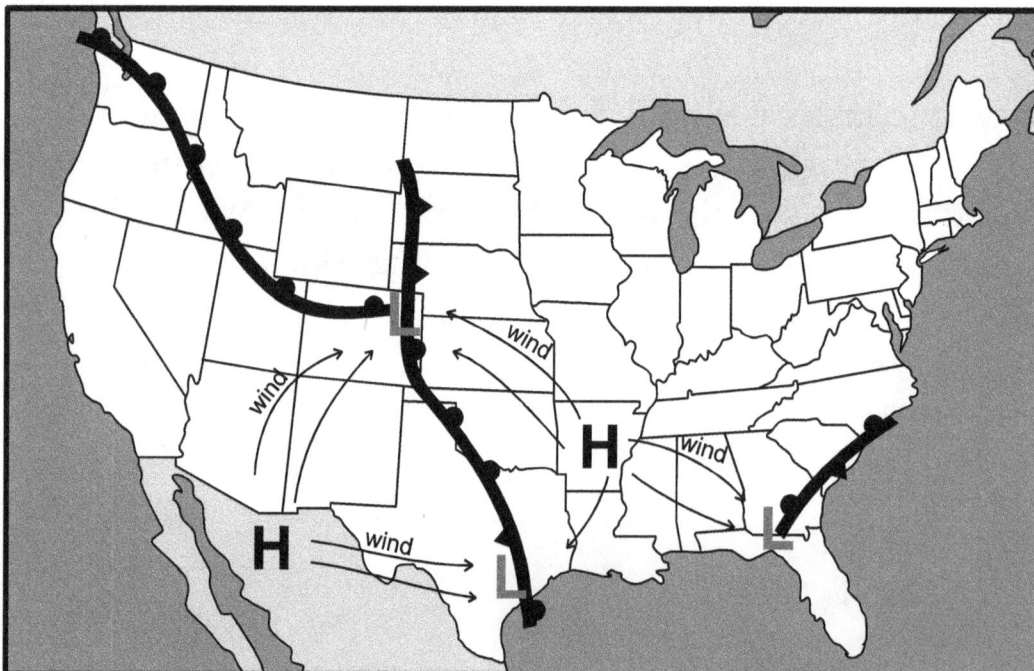

MAP 2   Same map as Map 1 with some wind arrows drawn in.

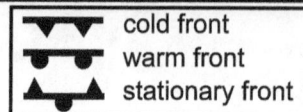

	cold front
	warm front
	stationary front

Storms usually happen in the low pressure areas, marked L on the map.

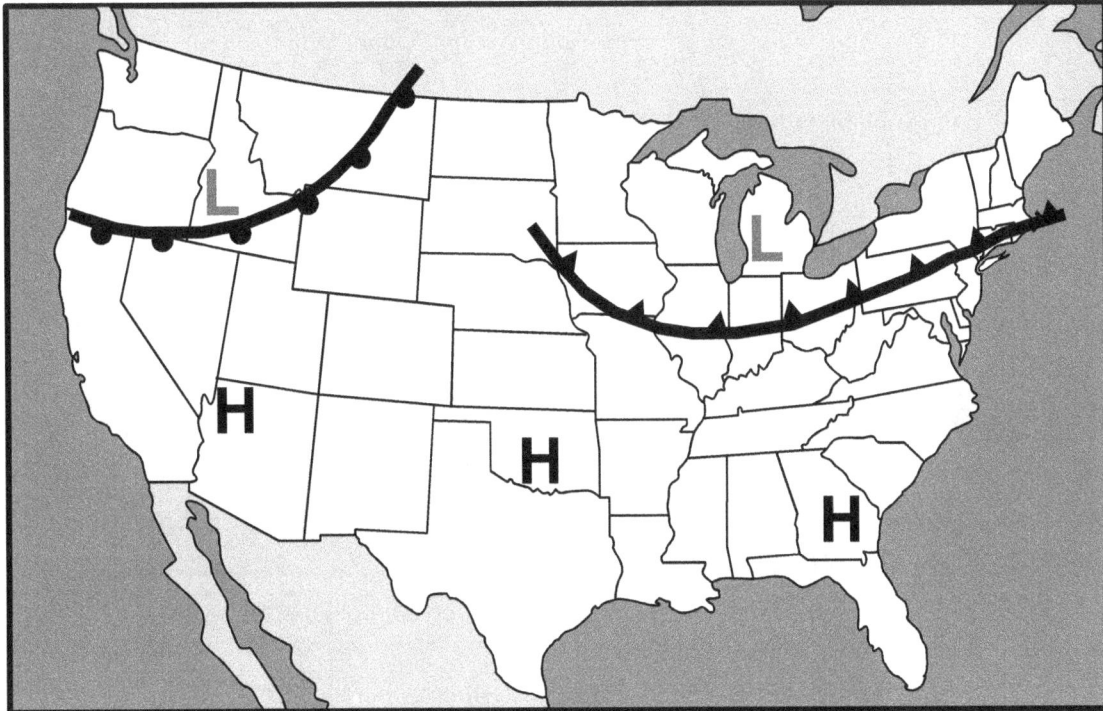

MAP 3   Imagine which ways the wind will be blowing.

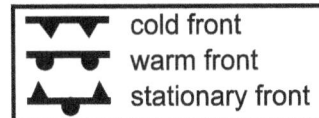

	cold front
	warm front
	stationary front

The reason for this is that low pressure air is often warm air (remember, it is rising). Warm air collects moisture from the ground. Then, when it rises up and cools off, the moisture comes out and makes clouds.

When the clouds cool off even more, the water comes out of them as rain, so you get rain near the area marked L. By the time the air has cooled off enough to go back down in the areas marked H, most of the moisture has already gone out of it. So the high pressure areas marked H are usually areas of fair weather.

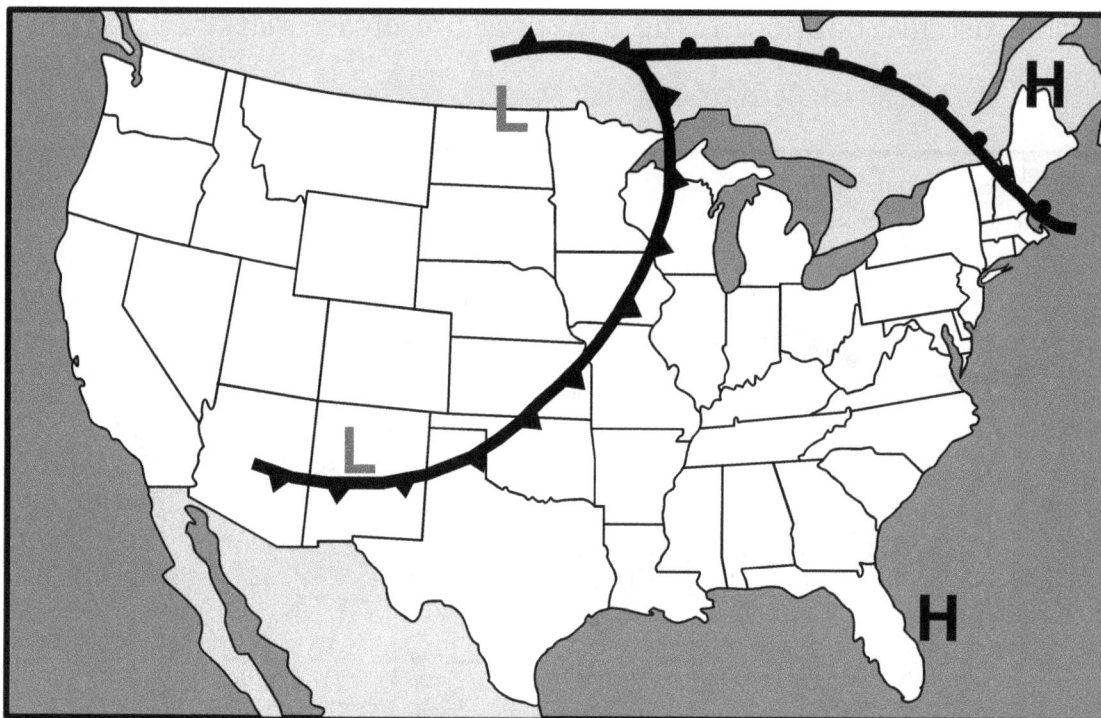

MAP 4   Where will the wind blow?

▼▼▼	cold front
●●●	warm front
▲▲▲	stationary front

LET'S DO THIS!

Predict Some Weather

To do this activity, you will need

- access to internet

Steps

1. On weather map 2 in chapter 15, show another person where it is probably raining and where it is probably sunny.

2. On weather map 3, show another person which way the wind is blowing and explain why it would be blowing that way.

3. Do the step 2 action on weather map 4.

4. Search online for "weather map cold front" or "weather map warm front." Find a weather map that uses the symbols you have learned.

   a) Point out to another person the fronts you see on the map, and explain what they mean.

   b) Show the person which way the fronts are moving, or if they are stationary.

   c) Show the person which way the wind is blowing.

   d) Show the person where it's probably raining and where it's probably fair weather.

   e) Pick a place on the map, and tell the person what kind of weather is probably coming.

Chapter 16

Using Weather

Wind is part of weather, and there are many ways to use the wind.

Besides helping us to tell what other kinds of weather will come, the wind is useful in other ways.

You can use the wind to fly a kite. It is good to know when there will be a wind if you want to fly a kite.

Wind can be used to run windmills. Windmills are big propellers that are turned by the wind. Windmills are used to pump water out of the ground for farms. Where the wind is strong and steady, they are even used to make electricity for whole cities.

Wind is important for flying airplanes. Airplane pilots must know a lot about wind. They need to predict the winds that go up and down as well as the ones that go back and forth. Airplanes can ride the wind to help get where they are going faster. There are even special airplanes called gliders that ride the wind and go long distances without any engine.

All the forms of rain are part of weather. Weather brings us snow. Maybe you like to go sliding. It is good to know when snow will come if you want to go sliding.

Without rain, there would be no rivers. If you want to go rafting, it is good to know how much water will be in the river. Rivers get big after a lot of rain, or when the snow melts in the spring. So when you plan a rafting trip in the spring because you know the river will be high, you are using weather.

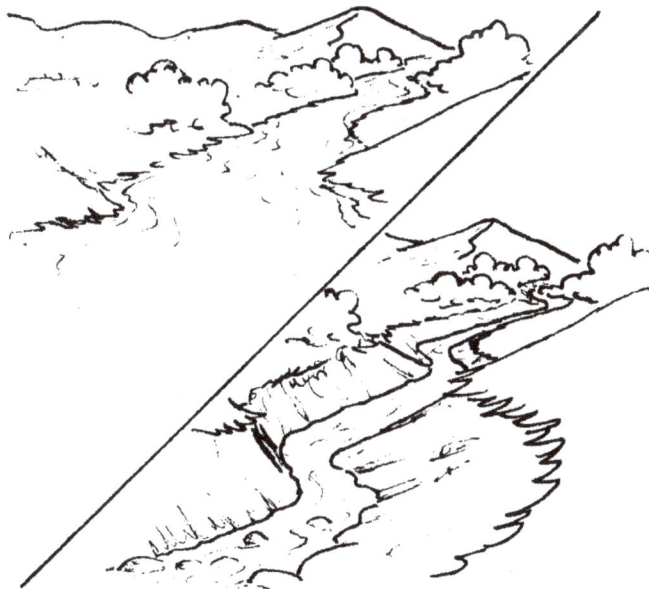

Rivers change with the weather.

Big boats that use the rivers for carrying goods must know when the river will be too low for travel, or too high and fast for safety. So they use the weather.

Big power dams that use the flowing river water to make electricity use the weather, because they too must plan for high and low water times.

Or maybe you are just planning a picnic or a day at the beach, and want a sunny day for it. You are using the weather when you plan for a day in the sun.

Weather is all around us, and we use it in many ways. If we can predict the weather, then we can use it better.

There is so much to learn about how the weather works, and how to predict it. Even scientists are still learning! But now you have made a good start into this fascinating subject of weather.

LET'S DO THIS!
Predict Your Weather

To do this activity, you will need

- your Weather Record sheet

Steps

1. Look over the wind and weather information you have written on your Weather Record sheet so far. Notice what the weather was like for each different speed and direction of the wind.

   For example, as you can see in this weather sheet, the weather was cloudy or rainy whenever a wind came from the east, and it was sunny whenever a wind came from the west.

Day No.	Date AM/PM	Air Temp.	Wind Type	Wind Direction	Weather Types	Cloud Types	Rain Meas.	Storm Types	Notes
1	Date AM		calm	none	sunny				
	PM		breezy	east	cloudy				
2	Date AM		breezy	east	cloudy				
	PM		windy	east	rain				
3	Date AM		windy	east	rain				
	PM		light	east	cloudy				
4	Date AM		calm	none	sunny				
	PM		light	west	sunny				
5	Date AM		breezy	east	clouds				
	PM		calm	none	sunny				
6	Date AM		calm	none	sunny				
	PM		breezy	west	sunny				
7	Date AM		light	east	cloudy				
	PM		medium	east	rain				

You can use this kind of data to help tell what weather will come next. Just looking at the data in this weather sheet, you would guess that when a wind starts coming from the east, it is likely to be cloudy or rainy soon. Or if a wind was coming from the west, it would likely be sunny for a while.

2. See what the data in your Weather Record sheet tells you about what weather seems to come with the different wind directions.

3. Show your weather sheet to another person, and tell what you found out about what weather seems to come with the different wind directions.

4. Have the other person give you different examples of wind direction, and you tell from your data what weather you would probably have then.

5. Show another person all your weather records. Use them to tell what types of weather happened on each of the days you recorded. Also tell how you did at predicting changes in the weather.

www.ingramcontent.com/pod-product-compliance
Lightning Source LLC
Chambersburg PA
CBHW080539090426
42733CB00016B/2629